FIRESIDE SERIES

# MAKING CONTACT

## OUR SOUL'S JOURNEY AND PURPOSE THROUGH LIFE

*JZK Publishing,*
A Division of JZK, Inc.

P.O. Box 1210
Yelm, Washington 98597
360.458.5201
800.347.0439
www.ramtha.com
www.jzkpublishing.com

These series of teachings are designed for all the students of the Great Work who love the teachings of the Ram.

It is suggested that you create an ideal learning environment for study and contemplation.

Light your fireplace and get cozy. Have your wine and fine tobacco. Prepare yourself. Open your mind to learn and be genius.

# FOREWORD TO THE NEW EDITION

The Fireside Series Collection Library is an ongoing library of the hottest topics of interest taught by Ramtha. These series of teachings are designed for all the students of the Great Work who love the teachings of the Ram. This library collection is also intended as a continuing learning tool for the students of Ramtha's School of Enlightenment and for everyone interested and familiar with Ramtha's teachings.

In the last three decades Ramtha has continuously and methodically deepened and expanded his exposition of the nature of reality and its practical application through various disciplines. It is assumed by the publisher that the reader has attended a Beginning Retreat or workshop through Ramtha's School of Enlightenment or is at least familiar with Ramtha's instruction to his beginning class of students. This required information for beginning students is found in *Ramtha: A Beginner's Guide to Creating Reality*, revised and expanded ed. (Yelm: JZK Publishing, a division of JZK, Inc., 2000), and in *Ramtha: Creating Personal Reality*, Video ed. (Yelm: JZK Publishing, a division of JZK, Inc., 1998).

We have included in the Fireside Series a glossary of some of the basic concepts used by Ramtha so the reader can become familiarized with these teachings. We have also included a brief introduction of Ramtha by JZ Knight that describes how all this began. Enjoy your learning and contemplation.

# CONTENTS

## Introduction to Ramtha
### by JZ Knight

*"In other words, his whole point of focus is to come here and to teach you to be extraordinary."*

You don't have to stand for me. My name is JZ Knight and I am the rightful owner of this body, and welcome to Ramtha's school, and sit down. Thank you. So we will start out by saying that Ramtha and I are two different people, beings. We have a common reality point and that is usually my body. I am a lot different than he is. Though we sort of look the same, we really don't look the same.

What do I say? Let's see. All of my life, ever since I was a little person, I have heard voices in my head and I have seen wonderful things that to me in my life were normal. And I was fortunate enough to have a family or a mother who was a very psychic human being, who sort of never condemned what it was that I was seeing. And I had wonderful experiences all my life, but the most important experience was that I had this deep and profound love for God, and there was a part of me that understood what that was. Later in my life I went to church and I tried to understand God from the viewpoint of religious doctrine and had a lot of difficulty with that because it was sort of in conflict with what I felt and what I knew.

Ramtha has been a part of my life ever since I was born, but I didn't know who he was and I didn't know what he was, only that there was a wonderful force that walked with me, and when I was in trouble — and had a lot of pain in my life growing up — that I always had extraordinary experiences with this being who would talk to me. And I could hear him as clearly as I can hear you if we were to have a conversation. And he helped me to understand a lot of things in my life that were sort of beyond the normal scope of what someone would give someone as advice.

It wasn't until 1977 that he appeared to me in my kitchen on a Sunday afternoon as I was making pyramids with my husband at that time, because we were into dehydrating food and we were into hiking and backpacking and all that stuff. And so I put one of these ridiculous things on my head, and at the other end of my kitchen this wonderful apparition appeared that was seven feet tall and glittery and beautiful and stark. You just don't expect at 2:30 in the afternoon that this is going to appear in your kitchen. No one is ever prepared for that. And so Ramtha at that time really made his appearance known to me.

The first thing I said to him — and I don't know where this comes from — was that "You are so beautiful. Who are you?"

And he has a smile like the sun. He is extraordinarily handsome. And he said, "My name is Ramtha the Enlightened One, and I have come to help you over the ditch." Being the simple person that I am, my immediate reaction was to look at the floor because I thought maybe something had happened to the floor, or the bomb was being dropped; I didn't know.

And it was that day forward that he became a constant in my life. And during the year of 1977 a lot of interesting things happened, to say the least. My two younger children at that time got to meet Ramtha and got to experience some incredible phenomena, as well as my husband.

Later that year, after teaching me and having some difficulty telling me what he was and me understanding, one day he said to me, "I am going to send you a runner that will bring you a set of books, and you read them because then you will know what I am." And those books were called the *Life and Teaching of the Masters of the Far East* (DeVorss & Co. Publishers, 1964). And so I read them and I began to understand that Ramtha was one of those beings, in a way. And that sort of took me out of the are-you-the-devil-or-are-you-God sort of category that was plaguing me at the time.

And after I got to understand him, he spent long, long

moments walking into my living room, all seven feet of this beautiful being making himself comfortable on my couch, sitting down and talking to me and teaching me. And what I didn't realize at that particular time was he already knew all the things I was going to ask and he already knew how to answer them. But I didn't know that he knew that.

So he patiently since 1977 has dealt with me in a manner by allowing me to question not his authenticity but things about myself as God, teaching me, catching me when I would get caught up in dogma or get caught up in limitation, catching me just in time and teaching me and walking me through that. And I always said, "You know, you are so patient. You know, I think it is wonderful that you are so patient." And he would just smile and say that he is 35,000 years old, what else can you do in that period of time? So it wasn't really until about ten years ago that I realized that he already knew what I was going to ask and that is why he was so patient. But as the grand teacher that he is, he allowed me the opportunity to address these issues in myself and then gave me the grace to speak to me in a way that was not presumptuous but in a way, as a true teacher would, that would allow me to come to realizations on my own.

Channeling Ramtha since late 1979 has been an experience, because how do you dress your body for — Ram is seven feet tall and he wears two robes that I have always seen him in. Even though they are the same robe, they are really beautiful so you never get tired of seeing them. The inner robe is snow white and goes all the way down to where I presume his feet are, and then he has an overrobe that is beautiful purple. But you should understand that I have really looked at the material on these robes and it is not really material. It is sort of like light. And though the light has a transparency to them, there is an understanding that what he is wearing has a reality to it.

Ramtha's face is cinnamon-colored skin, and that is the best way I can describe it. It is not really brown and it is not really white and it is not really red; it is sort of a blending of that. And he has very deep black eyes that can look into you and you know you are being looked into. He has eyebrows that look like wings of a bird that come high on his brow. He has a very square jaw and a beautiful mouth, and when he smiles you know that you are in heaven. He has long, long hands, long fingers that he uses very eloquently to demonstrate his thought.

Well, imagine then how after he taught me to get out of my body by actually pulling me out and throwing me in the tunnel, and hitting the wall of light, bouncing back, and realizing my kids were home from school and I just got through doing breakfast dishes, that getting used to missing time on this plane was really difficult, and I didn't understand what I was doing and where I was going. So we had a lot of practice sessions.

You can imagine if he walked up to you and yanked you right out of your body and threw you up to the ceiling and said now what does that view look like, and then throwing you in a tunnel — and perhaps the best way to describe it is it is a black hole into the next level — and being flung through this tunnel and hitting this white wall and having amnesia. And you have to understand, I mean, he did this to me at ten o'clock in the morning and when I came back off of the white wall it was 4:30. So I had a real problem in trying to adjust with the time that was missing here. So we had a long time in teaching me how to do that, and it was fun and frolic and absolutely terrifying at moments.

But what he was getting me ready to do was to teach me something that I had already agreed to prior to this incarnation, and that my destiny in this life was not just to marry and to have children and to do well in life but to overcome the adversity to let what was previously planned happen, and that happening including an extraordinary consciousness, which he is.

Trying to dress my body for Ramtha was a joke. I didn't

know what to do. The first time we had a channeling session I wore heels and a skirt and, you know, I thought I was going to church. So you can imagine, if you have got a little time to study him, how he would appear dressed up in a business suit with heels on, which he has never walked in in his life.

But I guess the point that I want to tell you is that it is really difficult to talk to people — and perhaps someday I will get to do that with you, and understanding that you have gotten to meet Ramtha and know his mind and know his love and know his power — and how to understand that I am not him, and though I am working diligently on it, that we are two separate beings and that when you talk to me in this body, you are talking to me and not him. And sometimes over the past decade or so, that has been a great challenge to me in the public media because people don't understand how it is possible that a human being can be endowed with a divine mind and yet be separate from it.

So I wanted you to know that although you see Ramtha out here in my body, it is my body, but he doesn't look anything like this. But his appearance in the body doesn't lessen the magnitude of who and what he is. And you should also know that when we do talk, when you start asking me about things that he said, I may not have a clue about what you are talking about because when I leave my body in a few minutes, I am gone to a whole other time and another place that I don't have cognizant memory of. And however long he spends with you today, to me that will maybe be about five minutes or three minutes, and when I come back to my body, this whole time of this whole day has passed and I wasn't a part of it. And I didn't hear what he said to you and I don't know what he did out here. When I come back, my body is exhausted and it is hard to get up the stairs sometimes to change to make myself more presentable for what the day is bringing me, or what is left of the day.

You should also understand as beginning students, one thing that became really obvious over the years, that he has shown me a lot of wonderful things that I suppose people who have never gotten to see them couldn't even dream of in their wildest dreams. And I have seen the twenty-third universe and I have met extraordinary beings and I have seen life come and go. I have watched generations be born and live and pass in a matter of moments. I have been exposed to historical events to help me to understand better what it was I needed to know. I have been allowed to walk beside my body in other lifetimes and watch how I was and who I was, and I have been allowed to see the other side of death. So these are cherished and privileged opportunities that somewhere in my life I earned the right to have them in my life. To speak of them to other people is, in a way, disenchanting because it is difficult to convey to people who have never been to those places what it is. And I try my best as a storyteller to tell them and still fall short of it.

But I know that the reason that he works with his students the way that he does is because also Ramtha never wants to overshadow any of you. In other words, his whole point of focus is to come here and to teach you to be extraordinary; he already is. And it is not about him producing phenomena. If he told you he was going to send you runners, you are going to get them big time. It is not about him doing tricks in front of you; that is not what he is. Those are tools of an avatar that is still a guru that needs to be worshiped, and that is not the case with him.

So what will happen is he will teach you and cultivate you and allow you to create the phenomenon, and you will be able to do that. And then one day when you are able to manifest on cue and you are able to leave your body and you are able to love, when it is to the human interest impossible to do that, one day he will walk right out here in your life because you are ready to share what he is. And what he is is simply what you are going to become. And until then he is diligent, patient, all-knowing, and all-understanding of everything that we need to know in order to learn to be that.

And the one thing I can say to you is that if you are interested in what you have heard in his presentation, and you are starting to love him even though you can't see him, that is a good sign because it means that what was important in you was your soul urging you to unfold in this lifetime. And it may be against your neuronet. Your personality can argue with you and debate with you, but you are going to learn that that sort of logic is really transparent when the soul urges you onto an experience.

And I can just say that if this is what you want to do, you are going to have to exercise patience and focus and you are going to have to do the work. And the work in the beginning is very hard. But if you have the tenacity to stay with it, then one day I can tell you that this teacher is going to turn you inside out. And one day you will be able to do all the remarkable things that in myth and legend that the masters that you have heard of have the capacity to do. You will be able to do them because that is the journey. And ultimately that ability is singularly the reality of a God awakening in human form.

Now that is my journey and it has been my journey all of my life. And if it wasn't important and if it wasn't what it was, I certainly wouldn't be living in oblivion most of the year for the sake of having a few people come and have a New Age experience. This is far greater than a New Age experience. And I should also say that it is far more important than the ability to meditate or the ability to do yoga. It is about changing consciousness all through our lives on every point and to be able to unhinge and unlimit our minds so that we can be all we can be.

You should also know that what I have learned is we can only demonstrate what we are capable of demonstrating. And if you would say, well, what is blocking me from doing that, the only block that we have is our lack to surrender, our ability to surrender, our ability to allow, and our ability to support ourself even in the face of our own neurological or neuronet doubt. If you can support yourself through doubt, then you will make the breakthrough because that is the only block that stands in your way. And one day you are going to do all these things and get to see all the things that I have seen and been allowed to see.

So I just wanted to come out here and show you that I exist and that I love what I do and that I hope that you are learning from this teacher and, more importantly, I hope you continue with it.

— *JZ Knight*

# Our Soul's Mission and Genetic Evolution

I salute you from the Lord God of my being to the Lord God of your being. Let us have a drink together this fine morn.

O my beloved God,
of that which I desire,
fill me
to all eternity
of the adventure of life.
I swear
I shall not pass away
but shall live forever
in the Spirit
of your bosom.
God help my life.
So be it.
To life.

Those are considered righteous moments. It is where you have lifted your love with divine focus above the tribulations of your humanity, and that is what allows the soul and the Spirit and, finally, the body to soar in what is called a state of bliss. If you missed it, we are regretful.

Well, let us begin this day's, this fine morning's teaching, a lesson that we will not regard it as the truth; we will regard it as a philosophy, including biology, neurology. And then when we are finished with this lesson, we will come to some suppositions in regard to it. But along the way what will become apparent to many of you sitting in the audience is — if you are peppered with the teaching — is that it will start to strike chords in you, and the chords we call a harmonic.

You are only going to be able to relate to this teaching if it is relative to what you are. The resonant frequency of the teaching will be a harmonic to you, and you will say, "That explains me exactly; that is what I am doing." If this does not resonate a harmonic with you, it is either because you are not listening, you are prideful, you are not humble, or you simply can't hear. I will give you room to have excuses.

What we are going to study today we have studied, as it were, over a period of time, a procession of time, if you will. And we are endeavoring today to tie and link it together in a procession, that we can in the final analysis discuss the enigma of the soul and the mystery of the body and come to some answers as to what a soul is, its most singular purpose for reincarnation, and what is to be gained from life.

How does the body that you come back in in the womb, how does the body influence the soul's future behavior? How do they come together? How do we begin to understand that we are living a life of our biogenetics or we are living a life of our soul and Spirit, and to be able to determine the difference?

So we are going to begin then this morning and we are going to talk about that which is termed the enigma soul. And if you take a clean piece of paper — And the greatest symbol for the soul at this start is a book. And if you drew a book, and in the book — it is called the Book of Life, that is the title, your Book of Life — and the first thirty-six pages of that Book of Life are going to fall under the heading of "Involution: The Journey into Mass or the Fall of Angels." The Book of Life is a handbook, if you will, for purposeful creation, purposeful creation. The preface page to the first thirty-six pages will read: "Enacting the Creative Law; Fulfilling the Mission to Make Known the Unknown. Herein are recorded forever and ever the events and adventures of my journey."

So then the soul is sort of like the log, that each spiritual being, meaning from Point Zero, the first level of consciousness, must have a soul because the soul is what captivates consciousness into memorable forms. Without a soul it is not possible to progress. The soul therefore is the memory of the Spirit.

In understanding this then, if we visualize that the soul is a book, that the first part of its text is entitled "The Adventures of Involution," then we could readily understand how consciousness and energy created a slow time, distance, and space to the point that consciousness itself became heavy in the form of matter, and so then we have slowed time to a thick point of coagulation. Our journey is to not only create this slowed time but to manipulate the matter of consciousness and energy in the form of physical atmosphere and to form it into models that we call life. We then create in this thick, slow vacuum models of life and potential that allow us to fulfill the preference of our soul, which is to be cocreators with God and to make known the unknown, to create, set it up for an experience, and then dissolve the creation so that energy can be re-formulated into a more advanced model from the last.

An example of that would be if you were to draw pictures of human forms of antiquity and draw them from that which is termed an apelike humanoid appearance and if slowly over the arrow of time you could see that through epics this creature starts to change and become that which is called the Homo erectus of today. That then is a great visual model to see that in the beginning it was our job to clothe ourself in thick time, which we call matter, and then in that clothing to interact in the environment and create models of that environment for the experience of creation. And when the past becomes the past is when it is no longer useful. When it is no longer useful, it was our job as Gods to then dissolve the past creation and re-formulate it into a new model that challenges us to always a point of what we call re-formation — re-form-ation — to re-form it to even greater. When we have re-formed the lifeform into a yet more sophisticated model, we then create for ourself a challenging experience. When we have created the environment that matches our mind to the environment and we experience it in this level, it then becomes the procession of the past, of which then we as Gods are responsible in dissolving that procession of the past so that we can resurrect it from dead into life again and create it even a more sophisticated re-formation of the past. Do you understand?

Now this wonderful journey is so that we may have all eternity in which to re-form life, and by doing so re-form ourselves. Now were we not perfect when we all descended? Perfection is a limitation and if it is ever reached, it will soon become imperfect because the mind always surpasses it. Do you understand? So to ask from a childlike point a question, "why did we have to fall if we were already perfect," we did not fall out of grace but through grace. Indeed falling was not a sin but rather an obligation, and that to carry forward the mind of God into the depths of creative potential is why we are here. We are as bees in the hive. We are working for the re-formation of the hive itself. Understand?

## ✗ Learning How to Distinguish the Voice of Our Spirit

Now the soul allows us a conscious review. The Spirit of what we are is consciousness flowing into energy, captivated in strata of mind. Those strata of mind contain the mysteries of the seven-level Fall in the very beginning. The soul is what crystallizes the moment for all eternity.

Now without the soul we have no direction in which to operate and indeed to function. Our soul is our log and our handbook. We refer to our soul when we are in need for re-formation.

Now when you have been told in the past to seek your own counsel to find out what your Spirit says, what the

Spirit of your consciousness tells you to do, it is called listening to that one small voice. And what the voice is is an energy input. The energy input is actually being given to you by your soul and it is giving you the direction in which you are to follow. It is the road map.

If you didn't have that, you would fall into carnal disgrace, dis-grace. Carnal disgrace simply means that we allow the only reality to be that which our body dictates to us to be. That is becoming the carnal animal. The body is animalistic; it must be in order to live in the kingdom of nature. When we fall into disgrace, it simply means that we follow the instincts of our genetics rather than the soul urgings of our own journey. This can be then complicated, because how does one listen for one's soul? And how does one discern the difference between the brain simply replaying its thoughts or the soul communicating to you and telling you which way to go?

The soul then is our packet that we carry from incarnation to incarnation to incarnation. Every lifetime that we emerge into, we carry the soul's packet with us. The soul allows us to engage beyond the disgrace of our genetics. At the end of every life we get to review our past incarnation, and we are weighed according to that. And who does the weighing? The God weighs the soul against the body. The soul gets to play out what it was allowed to create and re-form.

If the soul is allowed to reach one point of re-formation — which, remember, re-formation is the re-forming of the past. And how is that possible? Perhaps all of your life you live by the instincts of your carnal nature and that all of your environment is based upon your carnal nature. You give and take with people based on your carnal nature, and then right before you die something happens that allows you to respond transcendent of the carnal nature, and in that one moment — we call that the moment of truth — that is the moment or the hour of the soul. Then we respond not from the stagnation of our body but we re-form the approval of our body, and that is called the hour of the soul.

And when an entity's body perishes, what we are looking forward to in our review of our soul's life is to find out how well we were able to dissolve what is useless in this kingdom and to resurrect it up and re-form it for a new paradigm, a new model, a new thought. That is what we are looking for, because our journey here is not to cling to the past but to release it. Our journey here is like conquerors. We are here to conquer and if we conquer according to our soul rather than our body, we will conquer the human body. And when we have done so and impregnated our soul over and above the nature of our body, if our soul has its influence over our carnal nature, then we can pass the legacy of our genetics in the form of a new body. We take from our sperm and our ovum and we put it together and we create and re-form a body out of the ashes of our own, because the soul that we developed in our lifetime will be passed on as a new genetic form to the next lifetime. Now we have given back to the seed of humanity greater than when we came. It is called the procession of re-formation.

# THE SOUL IS AFTER CONTROVERSY, CHANGE

Now before we go into this, this is a preface to this work. A culture: This is the Western culture that we are meeting in the midst of today. There is a Southern culture, an Eastern culture, a Northern culture. And these cultures are what make the Earth beautiful, because the Earth should be viewed as a garden, and not a garden of the same flowers, because the sameness is equal to stagnation, but rather the Earth represents a paradise in which dotted around its landmasses are cultural beings. Cultural means the physical generation of a socially agreeable tribe, that the fundamental laws of that tribe are, number one, their spiritual laws in recognizing the divine in their environment and, number two, the laws of the tribe, which recognize a hierarchy that demands cohesiveness for the survival of the culture, religion, and law.

These allow then for a soul to come into a tribe whose whole culture is three hundred and fifty degrees opposite the Western culture and which would be seen by the arrogance of science as ignorant and backward. But why would a soul leave the paradise of science and technology and choose a lineage, a tribe, in which is utterly devout to the spiritual? Why would they leave behind white skin, blue eyes, blond hair, red hair, black eyes, brown bodies and go and become black bodies? Because the soul is endeavoring, like the dutiful scribe that it is, to record its journey in the form of re-forming the past into a body.

And so the soul may wake up from perishing as Einstein, it may wake up in Borneo being born to a tribal mother, delivered by midwives, a witch doctor in magic, circumcised, bathed in unguents that smell terribly, and having to be brought up very close to the earth. Why would such a brilliant soul who has re-formed so much end up in a tribal situation? Because the soul brings the opportunity to the tribe to enhance its culture — you understand? — not to destroy its religion or law but to civilize its religion and law; in other words, re-forming the tribe. Now why would a soul be interested in doing that? Because that then allows the soul to speak instead of the genetics to speak. Do you understand?

And many of you are this way today; you are very advancing souls who have lived as brilliant men and women, aristocrats and scholars, noblemen and noblewomen. You have lived lives of unimpeachable quality. And you know how you can detect such a soul? That they are usually born into a very predominantly genetically programmed family, a tribe — a tribe; family is a tribe — and though they have the propensity to be genetically like their tribe, they are absolutely different, and the difference is astounding. How many of you find this familiar in your own tribe? So be it. Isn't that wonderful, because in that difference there is an active soul energy that is more dominant than the active genetic energy. Do you understand? How many of you understand?

Now why would the soul want to do that? Because the tribe of your family offers blocks; the tribe of your family offers the mix of ingredients that challenges genetics to desperation — wonderful? — that that allows the soul to be born. Now this may sound rather indignant to you, but the soul is after controversy. The soul is a fire-builder. Genetics are firemen. I like it.

Now the soul begs controversy because only in such a battle is it allowed to engage all of its armament. You understand? The soul in reality is a warrior, a warrior that has ✻ As the Four Horsemen of the Apocalypse, it is the pale rider of death. And what it means symbolically is that the soul as a rider of death is that which strikes down the old, the civilized nature, and transforms it or re-forms it into the new nature.

So the soul then, a person who has an active soul is one who is by and large vastly different than those in his or her tribe. And though they have the same potentials genetically — you can say my brother is alike, my sister is alike, my father and my mother, and they all have this same alikeness from their parents, and you can see the filaments of harmony moving through each of your family genetically. It is very predictable as a line and an arrow moving toward sameness. And then if you see a person in a family who has the same propensities but argues against them — arguing, meaning that it is a restless soul who is relentless, never to rest, because when it rests, it will fall asleep in a genetic time pattern. How many of you understand? So be it.

Now this starts to happen. Some people have it — at the most — clarity, is right after birth that they are the most aware. They don't identify with their environment. They are riders of the wind; they are here to be a part of this environment. And little tiny babies are so conscious and utterly aware that even though the mechanics of their body cannot express as they will when they are adults, because the mechanics of the body are latent and unused, allows the soul to be more present at that time than any other time in the human life. And we will talk about children when we go through this.

Then there comes an opportunity in life. It is as if the soul goes to sleep and genetics take over. This is the norm for everyone that is reincarnated. And about the years of puberty — which are much earlier for these civilizations than in past antiquity — in puberty brings about the emotional storm of polarity, and polarity is defining men and women, girls and boys, in that the soul is utterly diminished and devastated because the body now is coming into the rightness of propagation, so the energy now turns into the serpent at the base of the spine and activates the entire human body toward procreation. So the soul then is utterly quiet and silent.

Later in life, particularly after thirty-five years of age, it is the dawning of the golden age in which that is the moment that the soul begins to be quickened inside of a human form. And it is quickened because the entity has gotten older and wiser. The soul has allowed the body to be foolish, arrogant. It has allowed the body to share its intimacy. It has allowed it to do everything. And then when it becomes older and wiser, there is one morning the soul starts to speak, and it is an urging. It is like someone is whispering to you but your brain can't make out the words. It is a propensity, an urging, an unsettledness.

Now the birthing of the soul can be as dramatic as the birthing of a body. The birthing of the soul has to break through the thick membrane of genetic heritage. It has to break through the thick neuronet programming that everyone calls attitude. And so the soul is being thrust up through the thickened layers of genetic/environmental/neurological training. So far the body has owned its territory, and the soul must be born in the midst of this territorial ownership. And sometimes the soul, very rarely, is born in joy. It is most often born in devastation; it is born in what we call the dark night of the soul. It is the soul's struggle.

And what we are actually saying here is we are talking about the urges of the soul, which is the memory of the Spirit breaking through, and it is a war that ensues. This war can go on through the rest of one's entire life. And who is battling? This battle creates manic-depressive people. It indeed creates depressive people. It creates unhappy people. It creates impatient, angry, short-fused people — does this sound familiar? — because in the hour of the soul and its birth, it is contradictory to what the mind-set of the human that it is occupying has become. Now is its hour to make itself known.

And individuals who can't seem to find any happiness — and there are many of those — who have fallen in and out of love and have been dislodged and only find that there is a large hole inside of them, the large hole is the ripe moment of the soul, because when the person comes utterly to the end of their own solutions and the end of their <u>wild animal instincts,</u> when they are broken and crumbled is the moment they give birth to the new heaven and the new Earth.

So what is then this dawning of the soul? It is, as it were, the moment that the soul steps forward and imposes its will upon the human brain and human mind of its host. It imposes a will that often means that the human being will destroy its past so that the soul can resurrect it. It is the story of the phoenix. That is what it means.

And what the soul then does, maybe will do only one bright and remarkable thing — maybe that is all it gets to do — but when its morning comes and it is filled with radiance and light and it gets to achieve, when it does, then the human being is bathed in utter peace, tranquillity, and bliss, because it has fulfilled its purpose. And <u>there is no money,</u> there is n<u>o woman,</u> no <u>man,</u> no <u>tribe,</u> no <u>culture, no religion,</u> no <u>God</u> that can bring such an ecstasy as the morning of the soul brings when it conquers through the encrusted form of humanity to do the work that it was sent here to do by its God.

*Involution*   *Evolution*

# THE LAW OF THE TRIBE
## AND THE WILL TO SURVIVE

Human beings have a countergenetic thread that runs through them, and the counter is that there is a great and powerful propensity of nature for its greatest species to survive, its greatest ones. So nature has instilled within its kingdom the strong will to live, the strong will of species survival. And in order for nature to continue to produce the environment to which the soul visits and re-forms, nature as a Goddess must always keep her kingdom clean and strong so that she may be intercoursed by God, the planting of the soul in the womb of her species.

Now nature provides a unique environment, that in this environment her will is dominant in all successful species for procreation and adaptability. Her species have ingrained within them the ability to adapt. Those that do not are destroyed.

Now in the civilized human, in its tribe culture, there is a powerful need to survive. That is the reason the tribe is built around a center nucleus that is both religion and law, and that the law is simply what the tribe agrees to uphold for its sustenance, for its abilities to survive.

The tribe nature insists upon conformity. Unless there is conformity, there is a breaking down of the tribe system. How many of you understand now? If we have conformity then, we have a tribe with spiritual recognition, tribal law recognition, and indeed the ability for the tribe to hunt and gather and to feed so that its physical bodies can be sustained and held together. If everyone cooperates in the tribe, then the tribe will flourish with crops, animals, through animal husbandry, medicines, social events, the bringing forth of children adding to the tribe's future, those children able to marry, to copulate, to bring forth more children so the tribe prospers. Are you with me? A tribe that does not prosper will be destroyed because they are only as strong again as their weakest link. Are you with me?

Now that is a very close and agreeable contract with nature. So it is improper for any one of you to say that any culture in the world is not conforming correctly, it is improper and it is also ignorant for you to say that, because all cultures in order to create the garden on Earth must have conformity as well as diversity that attracts the soul into those cultures.

Now this great string of survival is very powerful in the human being. The will for the human being to live and to propagate is tantamount. Now the will to survive means that you have to agree with the laws and religion of your tribe, and if you do, then you will be protected. So there is in the human element a need to come together and to socialize and to agree. There is in the need of the human element a need for leadership and law by which we become civilized and therefore become productive. That is tantamount.

Now this strength that binds humanity together can either be its salvation or its destruction. If the tribe does not evolve and become adaptable to change, then nature will destroy the tribe. You understand? That is nature's job. When it comes then to a strong-willed person we must then, not to be quick upon our judgment, ask ourselves what will is being acted in this human life. Is it the will to survive? If it is, that means that this entity is having problems with conformity in the tribe. His nature is to conform to be acceptable. His soul is counter to that. His soul is to re-form. Now are you understanding?

So now most people — and many of you in this room, all of you in this room — have had lifetimes to where your soul didn't break through at all because you were genetically housed in a culture that forbade clarity of mind and independence because it threatened the tribe as we know it, so you lived an entire life in fear. You had urgings but you never responded to them. So you went through the cycle of the human life: You were born, you were taught, you were ingrained in the law and in the religion, you followed the cultural demands of procreation, you brought forth children, you were a merchant, you were a nobleman, you raised your children in strict conformity to the law and to religion. And slowly as your life moves into its golden years, your wisdom starts to sparkle, but it is better not to do anything, for it is too late, and so then you die. So what has happened is you as a body got to have a wonderful, nonchallenging life. Your soul, on the other hand, was suppressed the entire lifetime because it did not add or change, meaning re-form its environment.

So what happens to people when they start to seek a spiritual life is there is a calling inside of them that feels like it is right here in the fourth seal, and it is. And the calling simply says, "I have done everything a woman or man could possibly do in this culture. I have traveled, I have laid with many men, I have laid with many women, I have drank, I have been sick, I have done this, I have done that," and what begins to happen is you begin to question then the meaning of your life.

Are you a villager? Are you simply a tribesperson? Perhaps you are celebrated in that tribe. Perhaps you are addicted to the tribe because the tribe all worships you or they all love you, and so to re-form the tribe would not be a good thing because then you would shake the foundations of love, or so you think.

When the spiritual life starts to call, it is the awakening of the warrior within, and what it is searching for is its life. And what it takes you to on your journey is to places and people that are sort of tribelike in their attitudes, except that the tribe is a spiritual tribe, but nonetheless it is still a tribe.

So on your journey you are looking forward to the moment that you are developed spiritually, but no one knows what that means, except that it means it is the moment that you leave behind the past and then you take the past and re-form it into the Now. And so when it is said that a genuine enlightened being leaves no tracks, what is being referred to is an enlightened being has no past because they have re-formed it into the Now.[1] Do you understand? So in the spiritual journey is a journey actually of the human being who finds itself in environments that may threaten its survival. And when it does it runs away, because its desire to live is greater than its desire for change. Soul means change.

Now what happens when you change and go back home to the tribe? The tribe is angry at you; you have broken their laws and their agreements and you are causing problems. The stability of the tribe is shaken by your obvious inability to conform. Do you understand? Well, what usually happens to strong-willed, surviving people is they go back to the tribe and they compromise. What they do is they take the lip service of philosophy back but they never rattle any cages. They are never going to change so much that they will be ostracized by the tribe. Do you understand what I am saying? So what they become is diplomats rather than spiritual beings realized. They have a desire but they are weak of body. They cannot move that body into change because its strength into survival is greater than the need for re-formation. That is why most people on a spiritual journey never make it past their family, friends, or the world's acceptance. They usually die in their miserable heap because it was their hour, and in their hour they couldn't give birth to their soul because it meant ostracism. It meant, as it were, banishment. It meant you were a sinner, you broke the law, you broke the creed of agreement in the tribe.

Now not too many people, I should tell you, are of such a will, such a spiritual will, that they can override the power of genetic agreement. And the spiritual journey

1 *Selected Stories III*. Tape 033 ed. (Yelm: Ramtha Dialogues, 1989), Story II: *Leaving No Footprints*.

then can be that you dedicate your whole life to trying to get the strength to move your soul. And you may never do it all of your life, but you could say, "In my life I pursued the spiritual life, but when I understood what the spiritual life meant, I did not have the strength nor did I have the courage to so apply myself, for I was afraid to my knees that I would lose my life, my wealth, my family, and my recognition." So then the soul vacates the body and we get to review the life.

## So What Is the Soul Looking For?

So what is it that the soul is looking for? It is there to fulfill the love of its God that says, "Remember all that you have done, because from memory we can re-form new lifeforms; we can mold them, thus we can create life as a changing circumstance in which we get to experience and create new galaxies of thought."

The soul then takes a look at that life and it realizes that it hasn't had an opportunity to be born to fulfill and to re-form, so then it is drawn into another body. If it is not very strong, if the Spirit isn't very strong but the personality is, the personality will be drawn back into another body and the soul will have little to say about that. And what it does then, it tries to be reborn in the seed of the womb. And working with its genetics, it feeds the energy of genetics, but at the moment that the child is formed, it infuses the child with its spiritual self of remembrance and the child has that for a while. And the child then must lay helplessly in the arms of its parents and try to hold onto its spiritual memory, the reason that it is here, while all along in the face of tribal parents there is an insistence upon denying imagination and becoming stupid for the sake of being a coddled pet. Does this sound familiar?

If the soul, on the other hand, moves out and it takes a defying point and turns its program onto the entity itself, now we have a war of personalities. We have a soul who is going to re-form the mind of its host, and that is its accomplishment. So then we have through life very troubled people. We have them troubled because we have a soul that is determined to re-form a mind-set for the sake of future generations. And why not? The soul may be looking that what it does in this life, it will be able to enjoy the fruits of two hundred years from now.

So then we have a life of sheer chaos, instability. We have a person who gets something and the moment they get it, they are unhappy with it. We have a person who can't even accept love because it is almost as if its soul doesn't want it to because if it does, it will go to sleep into placidity; it will drink the enchanted waters and will forget. It is almost as if the soul, like a storm, is pushing through this individual to a point that the only time that it feels love and peace is the birth of individualism. Now that birth is as powerful of a love as any lover you could possibly imagine. And when the birth takes place, then the soul has accomplished and been given from that human being a new genetic seed for future generations, for itself.

# WHEN BARBARISM AND COMPROMISE HAVE LONG BEEN LEFT BEHIND

The reason that you cannot become a Christ, a God/man or God/woman realized, until you have conquered this plane is another way of saying that you are always going to be a human/gross-matter species, because therein lies the conquest. You have not been at any other time since your Fall greater than the fourth plane. You have been mesmerized and ensnarled here. You have been the progenitors of cultures that have created massive stagnation. Your job is going to be the absolute re-formation of yourself, which will eventually lead to the re-formation of the human species.

And those of you who sit in this room and are hearing my voice on this tape, this does not exclude you. It is not inconceivable to understand that any or all of you could have been the minds who put together the Eastern civilization. Perhaps you were those who put together the Hindu faith. Perhaps you were the lawgivers of Egypt. Perhaps you participated in the geometry of ancient Greece or perhaps, even further, you participated in the power structure of Rome, and then to re-form the power structure perhaps you were the re-formers from Suetonius' Caesars[2] into the Christian re-formation of Rome. Perhaps you were part of that.

And if you were then, you can see how your work would never be done on this plane until you had re-formed yourself utterly and in the re-formation of that self could have freed the human being to be able to experience not the tribe of primitive culture but the tribe of dimensions of the human elements seen and unseen. It is a slow process to re-form against indignant people who must

2 Suetonius, The Lives of the Caesars, 2 vols., Loeb Classical Library ed. (Cambridge: Harvard University Press, 1914).

hold at all costs the tribe or the civilized culture together, because in that there is safety in numbers. It comes down to the fear of death. To go against the fear of death and re-form is a mighty act.

Look at how many cultures refuse to believe in the continuity of life, how many cultures refuse to accept that God is infinite as space is, has created civilizations markedly more advanced than this one. This would seem to be barbaric compared to the higher echelons of human species at their epic point of evolution.

Look at what causes closed-mindedness. Closed-mindedness is the symptom of civilized culture. It is the symptom of tribal agreeance. Closed-mindedness assures continuity. Open-mindedness assures anarchy and indeed the fall of the tribe, whether we see this in a family, whether we see this in a nation, whether we see this in the world. Closed-mindedness keeps civilizations together.

Now how closed-minded are you? What do you dare to believe in and what do you dare not to think about? What you do not dare to think about and find harmony with, your soul will press you to open. What you do not believe in is what the soul is after, the re-formation, to re-form a genetic line from being ignorant, which is the worst sin of all, to being knowledgeable; to assure that just because a person gains knowledge does not mean they lose control; to assure parents that if their child does not choose to go to higher education but chooses to see the world, to assure those parents that the child's journey into the world is equal to any education that does not provide experience but only philosophy; to get them to be open-minded; to allow the child to go with love and support instead of putting upon the child the fear of failure, the worry of contempt, and the embarrassment of what other people will say because the child has not followed the given tradition of conformity.

It is the job of God to re-form such ancient thinking and ancient modes of acceptance. And a re-former, a re-former never does harm but always has had harm done to them.

And who is doing the harm to the re-formers? The ones that are so afraid that the re-formers are going to do evil that they jump to do evil and to destroy an open mind and then call it a good act.

Re-formers are not to re-create the past. A re-former is one who is progressive in the procession of lofty thinking. A re-former is not one who is going to send you or your children back into the catalytic dens of concubinism. A re-former does not send people into drugs. A re-former does not send children into slavery. A re-former is to re-form the modes that allow them freedom, and their freedom will always be to seek the highest pinnacle. Freedom is not about descent but about ascent.

Now when we have such an astounding enigma in our presence, we can be assured that we are dealing with the God of that person instead of the body of that person. We can be assured that what we are looking at is a soul that is in control of transformation, and we should be in awe because they are rare indeed.

And the soul who is a re-former, as it were, is one that is both terrifying and awe-inspiring, because some of you say they are loose cannons. You know, a cannon that is loose on the ship, if it isn't tied down when the swell comes it will roll backwards and blow a very large hole into the side of the ship. Re-formers sort of are this way. So not only are they awe-inspiring, because it seems as if they move with the wind of independence, but they are fearless. And this can get you into trouble. But what kind of trouble? Ostracism, a downfall from a conclave — who once held you in a certain esteem — won't hold you that way. These souls are ones that when they finish this life, then they are peering at this life and they have ridden this horse of humanity superbly and they have left in their wake a modicum of change. Even if that change is through the child they bear or the people who witness their march, it will change them, and they know that. And they only have to affect one person. They only have to affect one person.

They then are growing in soul strength rather than humanity, and the next time they come in and they are born, so powerful are they in their Spirit that they have mastered the human being. They come back as conscious beings who are working through their soul, their Spirit. They are referring to their Book of Life in all of their deeds. They are aloft and always alone in this world because what is appealing to the carnal animal is unappealing to them. What they find beautiful and puissant is not what the human animal finds.

These people then come back, as what one would say, as prophets of God. They are angels of God. They are the incarnation of masters. And they come back and they have a life in which if in that life they need to learn the absolute re-formation of their own prejudice towards humanity, they will come back and serve all of humanity selflessly, serve and serve and serve, to give love and light to everyone that comes their way, or they may be the prophets that pass through a land, or they are the entities that are working for sovereign change of nature. And these entities often have nothing to do with the human beings at large but everything as far as helping them.

And so these are the human beings that we marvel at, who when they are persecuted and burned and tortured that they don't cry out or plead for their life because they already have their life — it is their soul — and they know that what is taken from them today, they will be able to re-create tomorrow. So rather than causing a dispute, they allow themselves to be persecuted, and in their nobleness hold forever what is truth. They are the re-formers of mind.

When that lifetime is finished, they come back then. They are solitary entities, and they come back as fully engaged consciousness and energy. They have completed their soul's journey. They have re-formed, they have struggled to conquer the flesh, they have given to humanity in the form of children, they have changed universal laws, and life in general, including nature, has been gifted by their presence. Now they come back, and this is the last time.

And they come back and there is nothing for them to come back for but to have lived a life without need, and they will do that. And when they live the life without need — Imagine a soul who clings not to its body. Imagine a soul who finds camaraderie in the wildfowl, who finds tenderness in a vulture, who finds a beautiful silkiness in an earthworm. Imagine a soul who feels the joy in the long thought of an oak tree. This is an entity who now embellishes all of life as itself, so then the focused identity that they are their body has been spread amongst the cosmos. Now we have an entity when they desire to go, they are not going to an uncommon place but rather they are moving to a place they already know, because they have unity in God. And when they do, they simply disappear. Their vibrations are raised so high, they go. They are not grounded here in the flesh of need. They have been free, and they are flying upwards. They are moving on.

Then they are reborn into civilizations that boggle the mind, of cultures that cannot be conceived, into another quest that takes re-formation to a greater, more prominent level, and have long left behind barbarism, selfishness, anger, have long left behind compromise, and have long left behind the need for human identity. Then their soul closes the book on evolution.

# In Conclusion:
## Two Keys for Viewing the Gift of Life

We then begin to understand how everyone in our life gives us two opportunities, whether it is our mother, our father, our brother, our sistren, our neighbor, our friends, our lovers, the culture as it is. There are always two ways to view the gifts of life: from a soul level or a genetic level.

If we then begin to understand that, then we could see that the reason chaos seems to move through our life is that it is the winds of change that are not brought on by genetic tolerance but soulful intolerance. And it is through these changes that changes the physical body for the next incarnation.

So everyone challenges us. If we have no one in our life that challenges us on all points of inquiry, then we are what is called peacemakers because the peacemakers actually cradle to them that which they are in agreement with, because the tribe must have conciliatory members; the tribe must have agreement. So if your life is filled with tranquillity, is it the tranquillity of your humanity or is it the tranquillity of your Spirit?

If you are the tranquillity of the Spirit, that generally says that you have lived in a box in which you have allowed only people who agree with you, only people who like what you are and you like what they are. Even the people you don't like, you let them live with you, because in that there is a love that humans have for judgment of others, and it is very important that they have people in their life that they can remind themselves that they are not. And it is usually that sort of smug indifference that happens that really is the instrumental action that destroys magic in a relationship.

Now if you have the need to dominate, the need to dominate is a cultural law. If you have the need to be submissive, that too is cultural law. If you have, on the other idea, an inclination of not preferring either of those, nor wishing war with those but to bloom as an individual, in your wake you will cause all of those things.

People who are unawakened have in their life foes and friends and lovers and all of that that keeps them in a box, and they remind themselves that unless they behave accordingly, then they are going to lose the box. But they are tyrants because they have psychic agreements with everyone in there that everyone agrees. It is a secret society. And if they disagree, then we have ostracism from the tribal secret society.

The soul knows this. And what happens when the birthing of a soul happens gradually is that we have an astounding simplicity of wisdom in the individual that seems to come from a very selfless/selfish place. The birthing of a soul is the speaking of wisdom, and a person who is wise, as we have now learned, is a person that is viewing life from the Observer and, we can now safely say, from the soul's point of view. And those who do that then have no attachment or detachment; they simply are. Now we have an emergence of the soul of an individual who does not need the trappings of human security in order to be wise. It is simply the soul speaking as itself.

We are not here to be a tribe. We are here to create and re-form. We are here to make known the unknown. There are many cultures that have existed on the Earth for ten and a half million years. Very advanced cultures that were extraordinarily advanced and beautiful came here when you were still not even hominids. They came, they did, they left. You get to reap the benefits of that. But the Earth has entertained extraordinary mind, extraordinary consciousness. And if we understand that then, we have within ourselves the ability to choose to be one who is embarking upon change rather than the cultures that now exist.

There are many people you say you would like to meet in the world. I should say to all of you that you have been all of the cultures in the world. You have been all of the cultures in the world. And if you were a true Observer and you went back and you could study the heritage of religion and law in each one of the cultures, you would find that it is very familiar with you. And you can even find that if you had a real propensity to be a very fleshy person, you would find yourself in places such as Babylon and Persia and Greece and ancient Egypt, ancient South America. You would find that you were a creature of comfort, and there have been many places you have gone back to because it didn't challenge you; it comforted you.

The Earth rotates in a cycle around the sun, and it takes many thousands of years for that to do that. In all the thousands of years that this one singular planet has moved around the full orbital degrees of the sun have brought about immense epochs in which souls who wish to be a part of epic change have come here and participated. The Earth continues to spin around the sun, moving through that which is termed degrees and minutes of arc, and it is there for the sake of moving into peaceful times and turbulent times.

The natural momentum of the Earth is to move through cycles of change that afford incarnating souls the ability to put their mind towards change in the middle of chaos or in the middle of peace. There is a fundamental reason for that which is called the equinoxes. There is a fundamental reason why the Earth has such a large orbit and it takes so long to complete and it is so slow, because it must offer to you, the evolving Spirit, the ability to not only create in times of peace and plenty but to be able to create in times of chaos and lack. So the Earth goes through its own biology of change, fulfilling its own natural soul need, and must complete that on its cycle.

There are those of you who will not have learned the difference between the soul's journey and the human journey, and you are going to be afforded a very traumatic and dramatic geophysical/geological/cosmological change that is now moving into place. And for that who listened and who heard and was aware and who survives it will then be given the gift of a new epoch and a new age that brings new challenges in the form of suitable survival and a coexistence with nature and its laws that are going to challenge even the most soulful of people.

Then why must you live through such a time? Because it is the soul's desire to do that. It is not the human desire; it is terrified. The soul is fearless. The soul searches for such epic times, that to move energy through chaos is truly the hand of a master, and that is what it is looking for.

And those who are washed away in a twinkling of an eye will find themselves caught up reviewing life in the sense of a culture, and seeing the foolhardiness of turning their back on nature and turning their back upon those who push for sovereignty and self-reliance. And the next time they come back they will be more conscious of preservation and more conscious of preparation because their instincts are that things change, and according to the swift laws of nature, that which does not abide by change will be destroyed and that which survives will be the select that will repopulate the Earth.

O my beloved God,
sun of my being,
I do give thanks this day
for this that I have learned,
for I celebrate this knowledge
as my freedom,
for I align myself
with my body
only through my Spirit.
God resurrect my Spirit.
So be it.
To life.

# RAMTHA'S GLOSSARY

**Analogical.** Being analogical means living in the Now. It is the creative moment and is outside of time, the past, and the emotions.

**Analogical mind.** Analogical mind means one mind. It is the result of the alignment of primary consciousness and secondary consciousness, the Observer and the personality. The fourth, fifth, sixth, and seventh seals of the body are opened in this state of mind. The bands spin in opposite directions, like a wheel within a wheel, creating a powerful vortex that allows the thoughts held in the frontal lobe to coagulate and manifest.

**Bands, the.** The bands are the two sets of seven frequencies that surround the human body and hold it together. Each of the seven frequency layers of each band corresponds to the seven seals of seven levels of consciousness in the human body. The bands are the auric field that allow the processes of binary and analogical mind.

**Binary mind.** This term means two minds. It is the mind produced by accessing the knowledge of the human personality and the physical body without accessing our deep subconscious mind. Binary mind relies solely on the knowledge, perception, and thought processes of the neocortex and the first three seals. The fourth, fifth, sixth, and seventh seals remain closed in this state of mind.

**Blue Body®.** It is the body that belongs to the fourth plane of existence, the bridge consciousness, and the ultraviolet frequency band. The Blue Body® is the lord over the lightbody and the physical plane.

**Blue Body® Dance.** It is a discipline taught by Ramtha in which the students lift their conscious awareness to the consciousness of the fourth plane. This discipline allows the Blue Body® to be accessed and the fourth seal to be opened.

**Blue Body® Healing.** It is a discipline taught by Ramtha in which the students lift their conscious awareness to the consciousness of the fourth plane and the Blue Body® for the purpose of healing or changing the physical body.

**Blue webs.** The blue webs represent the basic structure at a subtle level of the physical body. It is the invisible skeletal structure of the physical realm vibrating at the level of ultraviolet frequency.

**Body/mind consciousness.** Body/mind consciousness is the consciousness that belongs to the physical plane and the human body.

**Book of Life.** Ramtha refers to the soul as the Book of Life, where the whole journey of involution and evolution of each individual is recorded in the form of wisdom.

**C&E$^{SM}$ = R.** Consciousness and energy create the nature of reality.

**C&E$^{SM}$.** Abbreviation of Consciousness & Energy$^{SM}$. This is the service mark of the fundamental discipline of manifestation and the raising of consciousness taught in Ramtha's School of Enlightenment. Through this discipline the students learn to create an analogical state of mind, open up their higher seals, and create reality from the Void. A Beginning C&E$^{SM}$ Workshop is the name of the introductory workshop for beginning students in which they learn the fundamental concepts and disciplines of Ramtha's teachings. The teachings of the Beginning C&E$^{SM}$ Workshop can be found in *Ramtha: A Beginner's Guide to Creating Reality,* revised and expanded ed. (Yelm: JZK Publishing, a division of JZK, Inc., 2000), and in *Ramtha: Creating Personal Reality,* Video ed. (Yelm: JZK Publishing, a division of JZK, Inc., 1998).

**Christwalk.** The Christwalk is a discipline designed by Ramtha in which the student learns to walk very slowly being acutely aware. In this discipline the students learn to manifest, with each step they take, the mind of a Christ.

**Consciousness.** Consciousness is the child who was born from the Void's contemplation of itself. It is the essence and fabric of all being. Everything that exists originated in consciousness and manifested outwardly through its handmaiden energy. A stream of consciousness refers to the continuum of the mind of God.

**Consciousness and energy.** Consciousness and energy are the dynamic force of creation and are inextricably combined. Everything that exists originated in consciousness and manifested through the modulation of its energy impact into mass.

**Disciplines of the Great Work.** Ramtha's School of Ancient Wisdom is dedicated to the Great Work. The disciplines of the Great Work practiced in Ramtha's School of Enlightenment are all designed in their entirety by Ramtha. These practices are powerful initiations where the student has the opportunity to apply and experience firsthand the teachings of Ramtha.

**Emotional body.** The emotional body is the collection of past emotions, attitudes, and electrochemical patterns that make up the brain's neuronet and define the human personality of an individual. Ramtha describes it as the seduction of the unenlightened. It is the reason for cyclical reincarnation.

**Emotions.** An emotion is the physical, biochemical effect of an experience. Emotions belong to the past, for they are the expression of experiences that are already known and mapped in the neuropathways of the brain.

**Energy.** Energy is the counterpart of consciousness. All consciousness carries with it a dynamic energy impact, radiation, or natural expression of itself. Likewise, all forms of energy carry with it a consciousness that defines it.

**Enlightenment.** Enlightenment is the full realization of the human person, the attainment of immortality, and unlimited mind. It is the result of raising the kundalini energy sitting at the base of the spine to the seventh seal that opens the dormant parts of the brain. When the energy penetrates the lower cerebellum and the midbrain, and the subconscious mind is opened, the individual experiences a blinding flash of light called enlightenment.

**Evolution.** Evolution is the journey back home from the slowest levels of frequency and mass to the highest levels of consciousness and Point Zero.

**Fieldwork[SM].** Fieldwork[SM] is one of the fundamental disciplines of Ramtha's School of Enlightenment. The students are taught to create a symbol of something they want to know and experience and draw it on a paper card. These cards are placed with the blank side facing out on the fence rails of a large field. The students blindfold themselves and focus on their symbol, allowing their body to walk freely to find their card through the application of the law of consciousness and energy and analogical mind.

**Fifth plane.** The fifth plane of existence is the plane of superconsciousness and x-ray frequency. It is also known as the Golden Plane or paradise.

**Fifth seal.** This seal is the center of our spiritual body that connects us to the fifth plane. It is associated with the thyroid gland and with speaking and living the truth without dualism.

**First plane.** It refers to the material or physical plane. It is the plane of the image consciousness and Hertzian frequency. It is the slowest and densest form of coagulated consciousness and energy.

**First seal.** The first seal is associated with the reproductive organs, sexuality, and survival.

**First three seals.** The first three seals are the seals of sexuality, pain and suffering, and controlling power. These are the seals commonly at play in all of the complexities of the human drama.

**Fourth plane.** The fourth plane of existence is the realm of the bridge consciousness and ultraviolet frequency. This plane is described as the plane of Shiva, the destroyer of the old and creator of the new. In this plane, energy is not yet split into positive and negative polarity. Any lasting changes or healing of the physical body must be changed first at the level of the fourth plane and the Blue Body®. This plane is also called the Blue Plane, or the plane of Shiva.

**Fourth seal.** The fourth seal is associated with unconditional love and the thymus gland. When this seal is activated, a hormone is released that maintains the body in perfect health and stops the aging process.

**God.** Ramtha's teachings are an exposition of the statement, "You are God." Humanity is described as the forgotten Gods. God is different from the Void. God is the point of awareness that sprang from the Void contemplating itself. It is consciousness and energy exploring and making known the unknown potentials of the Void. It is the omnipotent and omnipresent essence of all creation.

**God within.** It is the Observer, the great self, the primary consciousness, the Spirit, the God within the human person.

**God/man.** The full realization of a human being.

**God/woman.** The full realization of a human being.

**Gods.** The Gods are technologically advanced beings from other star systems who came to Earth 455,000 years ago. These Gods manipulated the human race genetically, mixing and modifying our DNA with theirs. They are responsible for the evolution of the neocortex and used the human race as a subdued work force. Evidence of these events is recorded in the Sumerian tablets and artifacts. This term is also used to describe the true identity of humanity, the forgotten Gods.

**Golden body.** It is the body that belongs to the fifth plane, superconsciousness, and x-ray frequency.

**Great Work.** The Great Work is the practical application of the knowledge of the Schools of Ancient Wisdom. It refers to the disciplines by which the human person becomes enlightened and is transmuted into an immortal, divine being.

**Hierophant.** A hierophant is a master teacher who is able to manifest what they teach and initiate their students into such knowledge.

**Hyperconsciousness.** Hyperconsciousness is the consciousness of the sixth plane and gamma ray frequency.

**Infinite Unknown.** It is the frequency band of the seventh plane of existence and ultraconsciousness.

**Involution.** Involution is the journey from Point Zero and the seventh plane to the slowest and densest levels of frequency and mass.

**JZ Knight.** JZ Knight is the only person appointed by Ramtha to channel him. Ramtha refers to JZ as his beloved daughter. She was Ramaya, the eldest of the children given to Ramtha during his lifetime.

**Kundalini.** Kundalini energy is the life force of a person that descends from the higher seals to the base of the spine at puberty. It is a large packet of energy reserved for human evolution, commonly pictured as a coiled serpent that sits at the base of the spine. This energy is different from the energy coming out of the first three seals responsible for sexuality, pain and suffering, power and victimization. It is commonly described as the sleeping serpent or the sleeping dragon. The journey of the kundalini energy to the crown of the head is called the journey of enlightenment. This journey takes place when this serpent wakes up and starts to split and dance around the spine, ionizing the spinal fluid and changing its molecular structure. This action causes the opening of the midbrain and the door to the subconscious mind.

**Life force.** The life force is the Father/Mother, the Spirit, the breath of life within the person that is the platform from which the person creates its illusions, imagination, and dreams.

**Life review.** It is the review of the previous incarnation that occurs when the person reaches the third plane after death. The person gets the opportunity to be the Observer, the actor, and the recipient of its own actions. The unresolved issues from that lifetime that emerge at the life or light review set the agenda for the next incarnation.

**Light, the.** The light refers to the third plane of existence.

**Lightbody.** It is the same as the radiant body. It is the body that belongs to the third plane of conscious awareness and the visible light frequency band.

**List, the.** The List is the discipline taught by Ramtha where the student gets to write a list of items they desire to know and experience and then learn to focus on it in an analogical state of consciousness. The List is the map used to design, change, and reprogram the neuronet of the person. It is the tool that helps to bring meaningful and lasting changes in the person and their reality.

**Make known the unknown.** This phrase expresses the original divine mandate given to the Source consciousness to manifest and bring to conscious awareness all of the infinite potentials of the Void. This statement represents the basic intent that inspires the dynamic process of creation and evolution.

**Mind.** Mind is the product of streams of consciousness and energy acting on the brain creating thought forms, holographic segments, or neurosynaptic patterns called memory. The streams of consciousness and energy are what keep the brain alive. They are its power source. A person's ability to think is what gives them a mind.

**Mind of God.** The mind of God comprises the mind and wisdom of every lifeform that ever lived on any dimension, in any time, or that ever will live on any planet, any star, or region of space.

**Mirror consciousness.** When Point Zero imitated the act of contemplation of the Void it created a mirror reflection of itself, a point of reference that made the exploration of the Void possible. It is called mirror consciousness or secondary consciousness. See **Self.**

**Monkey-mind.** Monkey-mind refers to the flickering, swinging mind of the personality.

**Mother/Father Principle.** It is the source of all life, the Father, the eternal Mother, the Void. In Ramtha's teachings, the Source and God the creator are not the same. God the creator is seen as Point Zero and primary consciousness but not as the Source, or the Void, itself.

**Name-field.** The name-field is the name of the large field where the discipline of Fieldwork<sup>SM</sup> is practiced.

**Observer.** It refers to the Observer responsible for collapsing the particle/wave of quantum mechanics. It represents the great self, the Spirit, primary consciousness, the God within the human person.

**Outrageous.** Ramtha uses this word in a positive way to express something or someone who is extraordinary and unusual, unrestrained in action, and excessively bold or fierce.

**People, places, things, times, and events.** These are the main areas of human experience to which the personality is emotionally attached. These areas represent the past of the human person and constitute the content of the emotional body.

**Personality, the.** See **Emotional body.**

**Plane of Bliss.** It refers to the plane of rest where souls get to plan their next incarnations after their life reviews. It is also known as heaven and paradise where there is no suffering, no pain, no need or lack, and where every wish is immediately manifested.

**Plane of demonstration.** The physical plane is also called the plane of demonstration. It is the plane where the person has the opportunity to demonstrate its creative potentiality in mass and witness consciousness in material form in order to expand its emotional understanding.

**Point Zero.** It refers to the original point of awareness created by the Void through its act of contemplating itself. Point Zero is the original child of the Void, the birth of consciousness.

**Primary consciousness.** It is the Observer, the great self, the God within the human person.

**Ram.** Ram is a shorter version of the name Ramtha. Ramtha means the Father.

**Ramaya.** Ramtha refers to JZ Knight as his beloved daughter. She was Ramaya, the first one to become Ramtha's adopted child during his lifetime. Ramtha found Ramaya abandoned on the steppes of Russia. Many people gave their children to Ramtha during the march as a gesture of love and highest respect; these children were to be raised in the House of the Ram. His children grew to the great number of 133 even though he never had offspring of his own blood.

**Ramtha (etymology).** The name of Ramtha the Enlightened One, Lord of the Wind, means the Father. It also refers to the Ram who descended from the mountain on what is known as the Terrible Day of the Ram. "It is about that in all antiquity. And in ancient Egypt, there is an avenue dedicated to the Ram, the great conqueror. And they were wise enough to understand that whoever could walk down the avenue of the Ram could conquer the wind." The word Aram, the name of Noah's grandson, is formed from the Aramaic noun Araa — meaning earth, landmass — and the word Ramtha, meaning high. This Semitic name echoes Ramtha's descent from the high mountain, which began the great march.

**Runner.** A runner in Ramtha's lifetime was responsible for bringing specific messages or information. A master teacher has the ability to send runners to other people that manifest their words or intent in the form of an experience or an event.

**Second plane.** It is the plane of existence of social consciousness and the infrared frequency band. It is associated with pain and suffering. This plane is the negative polarity of the third plane of visible light frequency.

**Second seal.** This seal is the energy center of social consciousness and the infrared frequency band. It is associated with the experience of pain and suffering and is located in the lower abdominal area.

**Secondary consciousness.** When Point Zero imitated the act of contemplation of the Void it created a mirror reflection of itself, a point of reference that made the exploration of the Void possible. It is called mirror consciousness or secondary consciousness. See **Self.**

**Self, the.** The self is the true identity of the human person different from the personality. It is the transcendental aspect of the person. It refers to the secondary consciousness, the traveler in a journey of involution and evolution making known the unknown.

**Sending-and-receiving.** Sending-and-receiving is the name of the discipline taught by Ramtha in which the student learns to access information using the faculties of the midbrain to the exclusion of sensory perception. This discipline develops the student's psychic ability of telepathy and divination.

**Seven seals.** The seven seals are powerful energy centers that constitute seven levels of consciousness in the human body. The bands are the way in which the physical body is held together according to these seals. In every human being there is energy spiraling out of the first three seals or centers. The energy pulsating out of the first three seals manifests itself respectively as sexuality, pain, or power. When the upper seals are unlocked, a higher level of awareness is activated.

**Seventh plane.** The seventh plane is the plane of ultraconsciousness and the Infinite Unknown frequency band. This plane is where the journey of involution began. This plane was created by Point Zero when it imitated the act of contemplation of the Void and the mirror or secondary consciousness was created. A plane of existence or dimension of space and time exists between two points of consciousness. All the other planes were created by slowing down the time and frequency band of the seventh plane.

**Seventh seal.** This seal is associated with the crown of the head, the pituitary gland, and the attainment of enlightenment.

**Shiva.** The Lord God Shiva represents the Lord of the Blue Plane and the Blue Body®. Shiva is not used in reference to a singular deity from Hinduism. It is rather the representation of a state of consciousness that belongs to the fourth plane, the ultraviolet frequency band, and the opening of the fourth seal. Shiva is neither male nor female. It is an androgynous being, for the energy of the fourth plane has not yet been split into positive and negative polarity. This is an important distinction from the traditional Hindu representation of Shiva as a male deity who has a wife. The tiger skin at its feet, the trident staff, and the sun and the moon at the level of the head represent the mastery of this body over the first three seals of consciousness. The kundalini energy is pictured as fiery energy shooting from the base of the spine through the head. This is another distinction from some Hindu representations of Shiva with the serpent energy coming out at the level of the fifth seal or throat. Another symbolic image of Shiva is the long threads of dark hair and an abundance of pearl necklaces, which represent its richness of experience owned into wisdom. The quiver and bow and arrows are the agent by which Shiva shoots its powerful will and destroys imperfection and creates the new.

**Sixth plane.** The sixth plane is the realm of hyperconsciousness and the gamma ray frequency band. In this plane the awareness of being one with the whole of life is experienced.

**Sixth seal.** This seal is associated with the pineal gland and the gamma ray frequency band. The reticular formation that filters and veils the knowingness of the subconscious mind is opened when this seal is activated. The opening of the brain refers to the opening of this seal and the activation of its consciousness and energy.

**Social consciousness.** It is the consciousness of the second plane and the infrared frequency band. It is also called the image of the human personality and the mind of the first three seals. Social consciousness refers to the collective consciousness of human society. It is the collection of thoughts, assumptions, judgments, prejudices, laws, morality, values, attitudes, ideals, and emotions of the fraternity of the human race.

**Soul.** Ramtha refers to the soul as the Book of Life, where the whole journey of involution and evolution of the individual is recorded in the form of wisdom.

**Subconscious mind.** The seat of the subconscious mind is the lower cerebellum or reptilian brain. This part of the brain has its own independent connections to the frontal lobe and the whole of the body and has the power to access the mind of God, the wisdom of the ages.

**Superconsciousness.** This is the consciousness of the fifth plane and the x-ray frequency band.

**Tahumo.** Tahumo is the discipline taught by Ramtha in which the student learns the ability to master the effects of the natural environment — cold and heat — on the human body.

**Tank field.** It is the name of the large field with the labyrinth that is used for the discipline of The Tank®.

**Tank®, The.** It is the name given to the labyrinth used as part of the disciplines of Ramtha's School of Enlightenment. The students are taught to find the entry to this labyrinth blindfolded and move through it focusing on the Void without touching the walls or using the eyes or the senses. The objective of this discipline is to find, blindfolded, the center of the labyrinth or a room designated and representative of the Void.

**Third plane.** This is the plane of conscious awareness and the visible light frequency band. It is also known as the light plane and the mental plane. When the energy of the Blue Plane is lowered down to this frequency band, it splits into positive and negative polarity. It is at this point that the soul splits into two, giving origin to the phenomenon of soulmates.

**Third seal.** This seal is the energy center of conscious awareness and the visible light frequency band. It is associated with control, tyranny, victimization, and power. It is located in the region of the solar plexus.

**Thought.** Thought is different from consciousness. The brain processes a stream of consciousness, modifying it into segments — holographic pictures — of neurological, electrical, and chemical prints called thoughts. Thoughts are the building blocks of mind.

**Twilight®.** This term is used to describe the discipline taught by Ramtha in which the students learn to put their bodies in a catatonic state similar to deep sleep, yet retaining their conscious awareness.

**Twilight® Visualization Process.** It is the process used to practice the discipline of the List or other visualization formats.

**Ultraconsciousness.** It is the consciousness of the seventh plane and the Infinite Unknown frequency band. It is the consciousness of an ascended master.

**Unknown God.** The Unknown God was the single God of Ramtha's ancestors, the Lemurians. The Unknown God also represents the forgotten divinity and divine origin of the human person.

**Upper four seals.** The upper four seals are the fourth, fifth, sixth, and seventh seals.

**Void, the.** The Void is defined as one vast nothing materially, yet all things potentially. See **Mother/Father Principle.**

**Yellow brain.** The yellow brain is Ramtha's name for the neocortex, the house of analytical and emotional thought. The reason why it is called the yellow brain is because the neocortices were colored yellow in the original two-dimensional, caricature-style drawing Ramtha used for his teaching on the function of the brain and its processes. He explained that the different aspects of the brain in this particular drawing are exaggerated and colorfully highlighted for the sake of study and understanding. This specific drawing became the standard tool used in all the subsequent teachings on the brain.

**Yeshua ben Joseph.** Ramtha refers to Jesus Christ by the name Yeshua ben Joseph, following the Jewish traditions of that time.

**FIG. A: THE SEVEN SEALS:
SEVEN LEVELS OF CONSCIOUSNESS IN THE HUMAN BODY**

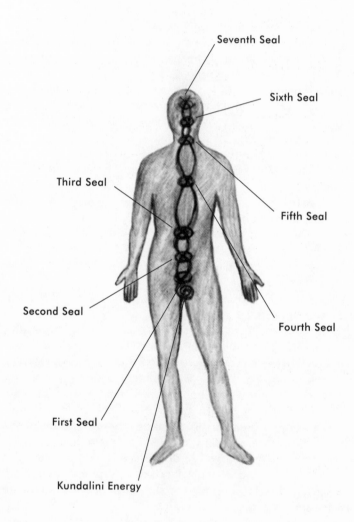

## FIG. B: SEVEN LEVELS OF CONSCIOUSNESS AND ENERGY

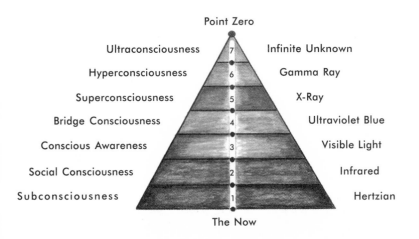

Point Zero

| Ultraconsciousness | 7 | Infinite Unknown |
| Hyperconsciousness | 6 | Gamma Ray |
| Superconsciousness | 5 | X-Ray |
| Bridge Consciousness | 4 | Ultraviolet Blue |
| Conscious Awareness | 3 | Visible Light |
| Social Consciousness | 2 | Infrared |
| Subconsciousness | 1 | Hertzian |

The Now

## FIG. C: THE BRAIN

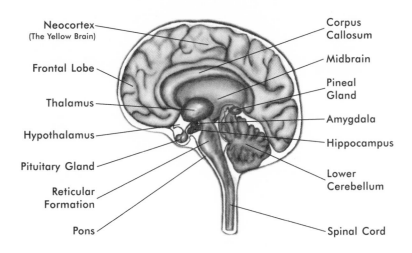

Neocortex (The Yellow Brain)
Frontal Lobe
Thalamus
Hypothalamus
Pituitary Gland
Reticular Formation
Pons

Corpus Callosum
Midbrain
Pineal Gland
Amygdala
Hippocampus
Lower Cerebellum
Spinal Cord

## Fig. D: Binary Mind — Living the Image

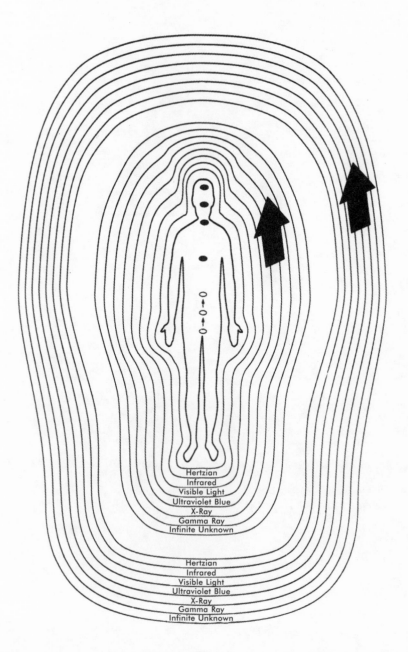

Hertzian
Infrared
Visible Light
Ultraviolet Blue
X-Ray
Gamma Ray
Infinite Unknown

Hertzian
Infrared
Visible Light
Ultraviolet Blue
X-Ray
Gamma Ray
Infinite Unknown

## FIG. E: ANALOGICAL MIND — LIVING IN THE NOW

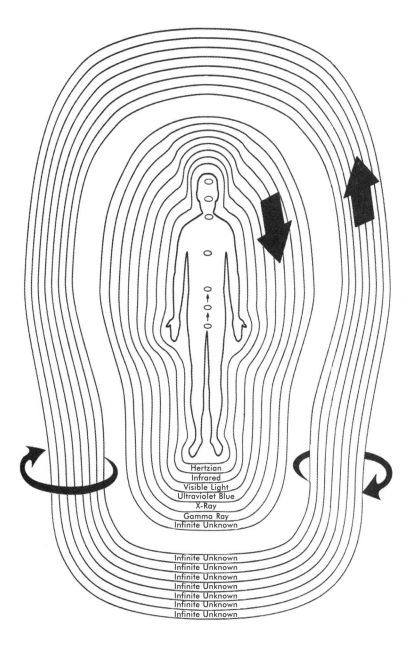

Hertzian
Infrared
Visible Light
Ultraviolet Blue
X-Ray
Gamma Ray
Infinite Unknown

Infinite Unknown
Infinite Unknown
Infinite Unknown
Infinite Unknown
Infinite Unknown
Infinite Unknown
Infinite Unknown

### Fig. F: The Observer Effect and the Nerve Cell

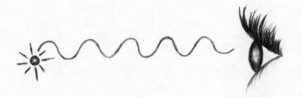

Particle               Energy wave               The Observer

The Observer is responsible
for collapsing the wave function of probability
into particle reality

### The Nerve Cell

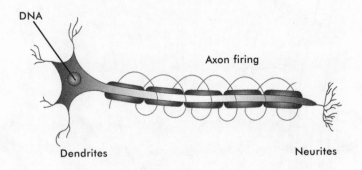

The act of observation makes the nerve cells fire
and produces thought.

## JZK Publishing,
A Division of JZK, Inc.

## The Library of Ancient Wisdom

## RAMTHA, THE WHITE BOOK

General introduction to Ramtha and his teachings.

It addresses questions on the Source of all existence, our forgotten divinity, life after life, evolution, love, the power of consciousness and the mind, lessons from nature, and Ramtha's ascension.

Many people became aware of Ramtha and his teachings in the past through this book.

Hardback
232 pages
Price: $19.95

## A BEGINNER'S GUIDE TO CREATING REALITY, Revised Edition

Account of important events in Ramtha's lifetime, from birth to his ascension, as well as Ramtha's basic teaching on:

- Consciousness and energy
- The nature of reality
- The self and the personality
- The Observer in quantum mechanics
- The auric field surrounding the body
- The kundalini energy, and
- The seven seals in the body

This teaching covers the introduction given to students before commencing studies at Ramtha's School of Enlightenment.

Paperback
238 pages, Annotated Edition, Glossary, and Index
Price: $15.95

## A MASTER'S REFLECTION ON THE HISTORY OF HUMANITY
## PART I, HUMAN CIVILIZATION, ORIGINS AND EVOLUTION

This volume tells the story of the origins of humanity before the creation of the physical universe and how we evolved into the first man and woman.

It also describes the genetic manipulation of the human race by other advanced races and how the ancient wisdom of our true origins and nature got lost and buried in superstition and ignorance.

The ancient schools of wisdom preserved the sacred knowledge for a future generation that would be equipped to decipher it and embrace it.

Hardback
368 pages, Annotated Edition, Glossary, and Index
Price: $29.95

## A MASTER'S REFLECTION ON THE HISTORY OF HUMANITY
## PART II, REDISCOVERING THE PEARL OF ANCIENT WISDOM

This volume continues the story of the human saga starting with the fall of Atlatia, Ramtha's war, and the fall of women and rising of religion.

It also describes a civilization within the Earth, their UFO connection, and the mystery of the pyramids of Egypt. A central chapter of the book is the story of Pharaoh Ra-Ta-Bin, who was the first human to stand up to the so-called Gods.

The truth about Jehovah, as the God of war and vengeance, is described in great detail. The book closes with Ramtha's description of the next stage in our evolution, the dawn of a new enlightenment.

Hardback
384 pages, Annotated Edition, Glossary, and Index
Price: $29.95

# THE MYSTERY OF BIRTH AND DEATH: REDEFINING THE SELF

This book explores Ramtha's teachings on the true self, the altered ego, and the mysteries concerning reincarnation and life after death. Now the teachings of *The Plane of Bliss, Part I* and *The Plane of Bliss, Part II*, appear together with other key, relevant teachings in one definitive volume.

> Paperback
> 230 pages, Glossary, and Index
> Price: $15.95

Some of the subjects discussed in this book are:
- Beginning the path to enlightenment
- The wheel of reincarnation
- The shadow self
- The Egyptian Book of the Dead
- The collapse of human consciousness
- Redefining the self as the spiritual self
- The dark night of the soul
- Death and near-death experiences
- Judgment Day and the life review
- The revelation of our ulterior motives
- The Plane of Bliss
- Mapping our next lifetime
- Genetics and the soul's journey
- Dimensional mind versus linear mind

# THE MYSTERY OF LOVE

"Love is not about giving to people everything they want. Love is not about physical seduction. Love is not about enslavement. And love doesn't have anything to do with owning a person's children. It is something else. And we shall study love today, something that my old teacher possessed an enormous amount of."

— Ramtha

> Paperback
> 64 pages
> Price: $6.95

## A Rockumentary

"This is for those of you who have been disheartened in the identity of Christianity, who have been disheartened in the identity of Islam, who have been disheartened in the identity of Judaism, who have been disheartened in the identity of Buddhism. This video is dedicated to evolution, and only watch if you are prepared to evolve. In the name of God — who no man and no teacher has captured the mystery of God absolutely — this video is dedicated to you. So be it."

— Ramtha

With his provocative message of truth, Ramtha goes *Where Angels Fear to Tread*. This film includes highlights from lectures delivered by Ramtha the Enlightened One to members of his school from 1999 to 2001 in Japan, Scotland, Italy, Spain, South Africa, Mexico, and Yelm, Washington. Ramtha is channeled by an American woman, JZ Knight, who was tested by a team of international scientists who unanimously declared Ramtha to be a verifiable phenomenon.

Drawing inspiration from the music of the sixties, seventies, and eighties, this is a rockumentary that will rock your soul into remembrance. In scenes never before viewed by the public, and with truth forgotten by the world, Ramtha peels away our personal hypocrisies and self-deceptions, revealing the lies propagated by world politics, world religions, and multinational corporations.

Outrageous, irreverent, and unforgettable, Ramtha confronts our illusions and beliefs and suggests that we ourselves are forgotten Gods and that divinity has never existed outside of us in any other being or deity.

"The world does not need another guru. The world does not need another priest. The world does not need another preacher. The world does not need another spiritual interpretation of the stars. What the world needs is truth."

— Ramtha

**W h e r e   A n g e l s   F e a r   t o   T r e a d**
A Rockumentary

www.rockyourmind.com

A film by Mark Vicente
Produced by Linda Evans
Length: 38 minutes

*Ramtha's School of Enlightenment,*
THE SCHOOL OF ANCIENT WISDOM

A Division of JZK, Inc.
P.O. Box 1210
Yelm, Washington 98597
360.458.5201
800.347.0439
www.ramtha.com
www.jzkpublishing.com